People with heart Problems in the BIBLE

Take A Journey Into The Hearts Of Some Of The Most Notorious People In The Bible And See For Yourself How God Reaches Out To Them With A Loving Hand

Lloyd Ortiz

PEOPLE WITH HEART PROBLEMS IN THE BIBLE
Take A Journey Into The Hearts Of Some Of The Most Notorious People In The Bible And See For Yourself How God Reaches Out To Them With A Loving Hand

Library of Congress Control Number:		2019910148
ISBN-13:	Paperback:	978-1-64398-949-5
	PDF:	978-1-64398-951-8
	Kindle:	978-1-64398-953-2

Printed in the United States of America

LitFire
PUBLISHING

LitFire LLC
1-800-511-9787
www.litfirepublishing.com
order@litfirepublishing.com

CONTENTS

DEDICATION

This book is dedicated to my wife of 43 years. Loving, strong, faithful and courageous are only a few words that could describe her, she is truly a woman of God in every sense.

"Guard Your Heart Above All Else,
For It Determines The Course Of Your Life."

Proverbs 4:23
New Living Translation

A Man Who Had His Heart In The Wrong Place

You have probably heard the phrase "That person has their heart in the wrong place". Well, this is a story about such a person, in fact, he was actually the first human being born here on this earth. We will need to go way back in the bible to the book of Genesis. In fact, we are going as far back as the first family on the face of the whole earth. The first two human beings, Adam and Eve had two sons. The older son was named Cain and the younger Able. The bible says that in the process of time these two brothers brought their offerings to the Lord. I don't want to get ahead of myself so let's see how this all works out.

Now Adam knew Eve his wife, and she conceived and bore Cain, and said, "I have acquired a man from the Lord." Then she bore again, this time it is Cains brother Abel. Now Abel was a keeper of sheep, but Cain was a tiller of the ground. And in the process of time, it came

to pass that Cain brought an offering of the fruit of the ground to the LORD. Abel also brought of the firstborn of his flock and of their fat (Best). And the LORD respected Abel and his offering, but He did not respect Cain and his offering. And Cain was very angry, and his countenance (Facial Expression) fell.

Genesis 4:1-5

I have no doubt that Adam taught his two boys about how to conduct themselves as they brought their sacrifices and offerings unto the Lord. Any offering unto the Lord is an act of Worship, so then how you worship him is of utmost importance to the Lord. Have you ever considered what worship really is? Jesus said this.

John 4:23-24

"But the hour is coming, and now is, when the true worshipers will worship the Father in spirit and truth; for the Father is seeking such to worship Him. God is Spirit, and those who worship Him must worship in spirit and truth".

Abel brought a sacrifice that was acceptable because he offered it in faith_.

Hebrews 11:4

"By faith, Abel offered to God a more excellent sacrifice than Cain, through which he obtained witness that he was righteous, God testifying of his gifts, and through it, he being dead still speaks".

People have the strangest ideas about worship, but I think that you will agree with me when I say if a person is going to worship the Lord he will need to worship with a right and good heart that is full of faith. Our worship to God must mean everything to us and it must cost us something. Worship is an attitude of the heart and has everything to do with relationship.

It's difficult to explain but a holy bond is created between a worshiper and his Lord, and that's exactly what Abel and the Lord had.

Hebrews 11:4 Amplified Bible

[Prompted, actuated] by faith Abel brought God a better and more acceptable sacrifice than Cain, because of which it was testified of him that he was righteous [that he was upright and in right standing with God], and God bore witness by accepting and acknowledging his gifts. And though he died, yet [through the incident] he is still speaking.

Cains offering to the Lord was not respected, in fact, it was rejected because the Lord considered it unacceptable. What was this all about? This is very interesting, but if you just keep reading a few more verses you will find the Lord trying to help Cain understand why his sacrifice was not accepted.

Genesis 4:6-8

"Then the Lord said to Cain, "Why are you angry? Why is your face downcast? If you do what is right, will you not be accepted? But if you do not do what is right, sin is crouching at your door; it desires to have you, but you must rule over it."

When you worship the Lord It stands to reason that the worship must be in line with how God intended it to be done. We should not just make up our own rules and expect the Lord to accept it and on top of that expect him to bless it. You see I believe that Cain noticed the blessing on Abel's life, so when he saw that God's blessing was being withheld he was not happy about it.

God asked Cain, "why are you angry and depressed if you do what is right and correct will you not also be accepted?" I believe it is in God's nature and character to bless and help people. God also told Cain, however, if you do not do what is right sin is crouching at the door of your life and its desire is to have you. God tells Cain to take the initiative and rule over it. In other words, Cain needed to take dominion and overcome this situation he was in.

Here are some fascinating things that the book of Jude equated with the Likes of this man Cain, he exhorts believers to contend for the faith that they had been delivered unto them. He goes on to say that some had crept into the church unnoticed, he called them ungodly men. You will need to read this just to see what kind of men these evil people were like.

Jude 4-11

"For certain men have crept in unnoticed, who long ago were marked out for this condemnation, ungodly men, who turn the grace of our God into lewdness (unbridled lust) and deny the only Lord God and our Lord Jesus Christ.

But I want to remind you, though you once knew this, that the Lord, having saved the people out of the land of Egypt, afterward destroyed those who did not believe. And the angels who did not keep their proper domain, but left their own abode, He has reserved in everlasting chains under darkness for the judgment of the great day; as Sodom and Gomorrah, and the cities around them in a similar manner to these, having given themselves over to sexual immorality and gone after strange flesh, are set forth as an example, suffering the vengeance of eternal fire.

Likewise, also these dreamers defile the flesh, reject authority, and speak evil of dignitaries. Yet Michael the archangel, in contending with the devil, when he disputed about the body of Moses, dared not bring against him a reviling accusation, but said, "The Lord rebuke you!" But these speak evil of whatever they do not know; and whatever they know naturally, like brute beasts, in these things they corrupt themselves. Woe to them! For they have gone in the way of Cain".

The people that Jude is talking about here are ungodly and wicked people, to say the least, the shocking thing is that Jude equates Cain with these guys. Was Cain a wicked man?

1 John 3:10-13

"This is how we know who the children of God are and who the children of the devil are: Anyone who does not do what is right is not God's child, nor is anyone who does not love their brother and sister.

For this is the message you heard from the beginning: We should love one another. Do not be like Cain, who belonged to the evil one and

murdered his brother. And why did he murder him? Because his own actions were evil and his brothers were righteous".

This scripture from the apostle John is self-explanatory, Cain belonged to the devil, or you could say the evil and wicked one. Satan is a rebel and Cain was a just like him in many ways. You see when God says something must be done a certain way Satan naturally wants to do the opposite. I believe that God had already instituted the way their sacrifices should be conducted. When Abel brought his sacrifice the bible says that he brought an offering — fat portions from some of the firstborn of his flock. God was pleased. When Cain brought his they were of a different sort. The Bible points out that Cain worked the soil. In the course of time, Cain brought some of the fruits of the soil as an offering to the LORD.

Without a doubt, I believe that the Lord had already begun the process of that one day when Jesus would become our substitutionary sacrifice. Here is something to think about. When God had called Adam, Eve and the serpent on the carpet because of their disobedience God told Satan that one day someone would come to crush the head of the devil, dethrone him and cast him out.

Genesis 3:14-15

"'Cursed are you above all livestock and all wild animals! You will crawl on your belly and you will eat dust all the days of your life. And I will put enmity between you and the woman, and between your offspring and hers; he will crush your head, and you will strike his heel".

Adam and his wife Eve tried to cover their nakedness with fig leaves, however, God in his mercy saw to it that they should be covered with animal skins, which means that animals would need to be killed so that their nakedness could be covered.

Genesis 3:21

"Unto Adam also and to his wife did the LORD God make coats of skins, and clothed them".

When Jude exhorted the church to earnestly contend for the faith, he was warning the believers of his day of false brethren who had crept into the church unawares. These men are dangerous, selfish and have no respect for the things and purposes of God. Note the characteristics of these so-called infiltrators, they sound so much like Cain. When God tried to help Cain, all he received in return was a cold shoulder and a disgruntled and resentful attitude. This was just one of the so-called ways of Cain. Well, I think you know where this is going. After the Lord said what he had to say the bible says that Cain rose up against his brother and killed him, this is another way of this man the Bible calls Cain. When the Lord came to confront Cain he was very disrespectful with God.

Genesis 4:9-15

"Then the LORD said to Cain, "Where is Abel your brother?" He said, "I do not know. Am I my brother's keeper?"

And He said, "What have you done? The voice of your brother's blood cries out to Me from the ground. So now you are cursed from the earth, which has opened its mouth to receive your brother's blood from your hand. When you till the ground, it shall no longer yield its strength to you. A fugitive and a vagabond you shall be on the earth.

And Cain said to the LORD, My punishment is greater than I can bear! Surely You have driven me out this day from the face of the ground; I shall be hidden from Your face; I shall be a fugitive and a vagabond on the earth, and it will happen that anyone who finds me will kill me."

And the LORD said to him, "Therefore, whoever kills Cain, vengeance shall be taken on him sevenfold." And the LORD set a mark on Cain, lest anyone finding him should kill him".

I would like for you to just take a little journey with me to the book of Job in the bible because there is something I want you to see.

Job 1:6-11

"Now there was a day when the sons of God came to present themselves before the LORD, and Satan also came among them. And the LORD said to Satan, "From where do you come?"

So Satan answered the LORD and said, "From going to and fro on the earth, and from walking back and forth on it."

Then the LORD said to Satan, "Have you considered My servant Job, that there is none like him on the earth, a blameless and upright man, one who fears God and shuns evil?"

So Satan answered the LORD and said, "Does Job fear God for nothing? Have You not made a hedge around him, around his household, and around all that he has on every side? You have blessed the work of his hands, and his possessions have increased in the land. But now, stretch out Your hand and touch all that he has, and he will surely curse You to Your face!"

I would like for you to notice some similarities in the way Satan disrespectfully speaks to the Lord and the way that Cain did the same. When a person loves God, he reveres and respects him deeply. We are talking about Almighty God here, the creator of all things. God is to be honored at all times. So then you can now clearly see that this is another way of this man Cain.

Cain commits one sin after another with no regard for man or God. He is boastful, arrogant, prideful and very selfish. After God pronounces his judgment upon Cain for his unwillingness to repent, Cain displays an attitude that we see all too often.

Genesis 4:8-16

"Now Cain said to his brother Abel, "Let's go out to the field." While they were in the field, Cain attacked his brother Abel and killed him.

Then the LORD said to Cain, "Where is your brother Abel?"

"I don't know," he replied. "Am I my brother's keeper?"

The LORD said, "What have you done? Listen! Your brother's blood cries out to me from the ground. Now you are under a curse and driven from the ground, which opened its mouth to receive your brother's blood from your hand. When you work the ground, it will no longer yield its crops for you. You will be a restless wanderer on the earth."

Cain said to the LORD, "My punishment is more than I can bear. Today you are driving me from the land, and I will be hidden from your presence; I will be a restless wanderer on the earth, and whoever finds me will kill me."

But the LORD said to him, "Not so; anyone who kills Cain will suffer vengeance seven times over." Then the LORD put a mark on Cain so that no one who found him would kill him. So Cain went out from the LORD's presence and lived in the land of Nod, east of Eden".

As I said earlier, Cain displays what we all see all too often when a person is caught in wrongdoing, and that is a spirit of selfishness. After God questions him about his evil deed he is only concerned about himself. Listen to what he said and how he said it. "***My*** punishment is more than ***I*** can bear,"- ***I*** will be hidden from your presence,"- ***I*** will be a restless wanderer,"- and whoever finds ***me*** will kill ***me.***"

Six personal pronouns are used in regard to himself in very brief and curt responses to God's Judgment on him, his concern is for himself and himself alone, not for his dead innocent brother Abel and certainly not for God.

The wise thing that Cain should have done is to admit his wrong and ask the Lord for his forgiveness.

Isaiah 55:7

"Let the wicked forsake his way, and the unrighteous man his thoughts: and let him return unto the LORD, and he will have mercy upon him; and to our God, for he will abundantly pardon".

This poor fellow was not willing to admit wrongdoing at all, he had his heart fixed and he refused to be moved, this was another way of Cain. The word of God was given to us so that we could be changed by it. Believe it or not, I believe God expects us to yield and surrender to it's transforming power, if we allow it to have preeminence in our lives, I believe with all of my heart that we will be formed and fashioned in such a miraculous way that we will never be the same again. Think about it, if you have read the word of God for any length of time at all you will begin to see a pattern of lives changed by Gods word beginning in the Old Testament and continuing all the way thru the New Testament. Peoples lives were transformed, people's destinies were changed, peoples hearts were changed, peoples names were changed, peoples minds were changed and then finally the Lord ultimately changes believers bodies themselves so that they can enjoy eternity with him. God will not be satisfied until he changes us so thoroughly and completely. Here are just a couple of scriptures that I believe prove the point that I am trying to make.

2 Corinthians 3:17-18

"Now the Lord is the Spirit, and where the Spirit of the Lord is, there is freedom. And we all, who with unveiled faces contemplate the Lord's glory, are being changed into his image with ever-increasing glory, which comes from the Lord, who is the Spirit".

1 Corinthians 15:50-52

"I declare to you, brothers and sisters, that flesh and blood cannot inherit the kingdom of God, nor does the perishable inherit the imperishable. Listen, I tell you a mystery: We will not all sleep, but we will all be changed— in a flash, in the twinkling of an eye, at the last trumpet. For the trumpet will sound, the dead will be raised imperishable, and we will be changed".

People that have a true relationship with Jesus have a different heart about them. God said that he would give us a new heart if we would just give him our hearts in true surrender. The new life that Jesus offers all that would follow him will have characteristics or distinguishing features that mark them as his children. These new people will be just like him in so many ways, Jesus said that a tree is known by its fruit. You see, a true and genuine follower of the Lord will show a positive and undeniable change in their lives.

I pray that this story about Cain would help you evaluate your life. Listen to this scripture in Proverbs 14:12 "There is a way that seems right to a man, But its end is the way of death". The wisest thing we can do is forsake our ways and follow the Lord.

Isaiah 55:6-7

"Seek the LORD while he may be found; call on him while he is near. Let the wicked forsake their ways and the unrighteous their thoughts. Let them turn to the LORD, and he will have mercy on them and to our God, for he will freely pardon".

Cain had his heart in the wrong place. His heart did not belong to God but it belonged to the evil one.

A Creepy Story About Two Women Who Shared The Same Heart

Have you ever heard tales of creepy coincidences? Listen to this story by **Cracked Readers.**

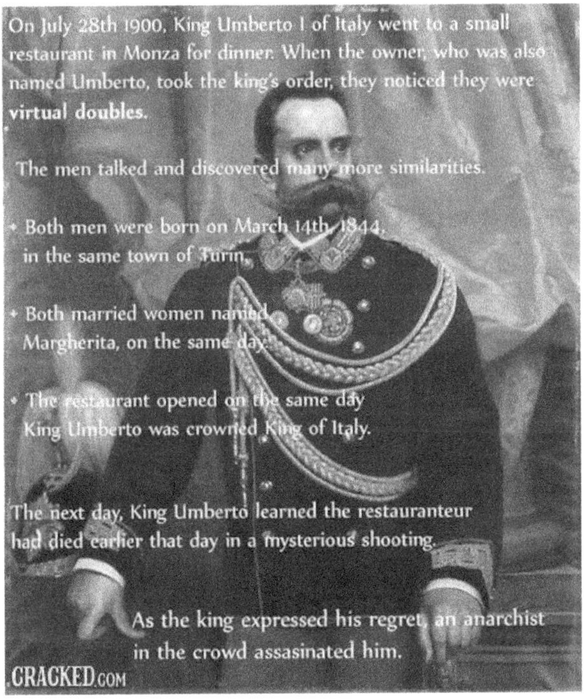

Creepy? Absolutely, however, if you look through the bible you will begin to find some incredible similarities that connect people lives or events; at least in the forms of what the bible calls types, shadows or figures. Creepy may not be the word that I am looking for but in many instances they sure are bizarre. So then, let me introduce to you to the first woman and explain a little about who she was and how she lived. Her name was Jezebel. If you don't know this character and what she stood for, you may be able to recognize her by some of the ways people use or don't use her name today. Have you ever met a person who was named Jezebel? I read someone's comment on an article called, (*Behind The Name*) and this is what they said, (Anonymous) "*Her name actually does have a pretty ring to it, but it still smacks of corruption and evil. A Jezebel (usually left uncapitalized) is usually seen today as a vamp, temptress, or any immoral or corrupt woman*".

You really don't have to be a bible scholar to get somewhat of an accurate idea about this person. I for one am amazed at how wicked people can become, I have seen some pretty bad people in my day and I have heard of a few people who were bad to the bone and Jezebel is one of them she is definitely considered a bad girl of the Bible. This strikes me as odd because people are made in the image of God and because of that, they should reflect or display the same image as their creator, however, in this case, we find that Jezebel personifies a different likeness altogether. Again, you don't have to be a bible scholar to see who this strange woman personifies, she reflects the nature of the evil one himself.

I use to love some of the elementary school activities in my younger days and connecting the dots was definitely one of them. So then, It's really not difficult to connect the dots between the devil himself and this woman called Jezebel. Jesus also saw similarities with some of the people of his day. In fact, there were more than a few instances when Jesus teachings were met with much ridicule and some major disagreements from many of his adversaries.

John 8:42

Jesus told them, "If God were your Father, you would love me because I have come to you from God. I am not here on my own, but he sent me. Why can't you understand what I am saying? It's because you can't even hear me! For you are the children of your father the devil, and you love to do the evil things he does. He was a murderer from the beginning. He has always hated the truth because there is no truth in him. When he lies, it is consistent with his character; for he is a liar and the father of lies. So when I tell the truth, you just naturally don't believe me! Which of you can truthfully accuse me of sin? And since I am telling you the truth, why don't you believe me? Anyone who belongs to God listens gladly to the words of God. But you don't listen because you don't belong to God."

Have you ever wondered how there could be such a contrast between the people that God created and God himself? The answer to that question lies at the beginning when God created mankind. To make a long story very short, when God had created Adam and Eve, the first man and the first woman, Satan found a way into their lives and into humanity through his lies and deception along with their disobedience. Since that day humankind has gravitated toward evil and corruption. Does this sound sad or what?

Since that day we were all born with propensities and tendencies that fall short of the glory and goodness of a loving God who created each and every one of us.

As bad as all this may sound, we are all still able to choose to do right or wrong or even good or evil for that matter. Evil is all around us but we don't need to give ourselves over to it, in fact, God has already made provision for us to be able to live good and joyful lives. He did this by sending his son Jesus Christ to suffer on our behalf and die for our sins.

I believe that Jezebel was controlled by an evil spirit that despised and hated God along with anything that God represented. This evil spirit has to have its way, and will do anything to achieve its purpose. With Jezebel, control was the name of the game. Jezebel's name means, Baal exalts or Baal is husband. Her father's name was Ethbaal. This families name had ***devil*** written all over it. You can follow the name Baal all over the bible and it comes up in different ways, from Baal to Baalzebub and finally, in the New Testament we see it as Beelzebub, so no matter which way you may find it, you will see that it always points back to the devil. As I said earlier, this evil spirit will use every means possible to gain control over people. If you just look back a few pages in your bible you will see this when king Ahab goes out and marries this woman Jezebel. King Ahab was a weak man in more ways than you may know. This was a perfect setup for disaster for the northern kingdom of Israel. In those days kings would make alliances with other countries as a way to receive mutual benefits especially if they had military interests, nevertheless, this is what King Ahab did with Ethbaal of Tyre, King of Phoenicia. This King (Ethbaal) was not only Jezebels dad he was also the high priest of their worship of Baal.

So now you can see that this woman had been raised and steeped, or you could say "strongly influenced" by this abominable deity that they all served, and by the way *served* would be a fitting word for them because Baal means (Master). Ahab being the weak man that he was, seemed to be a perfect match for Satan's plan of eliminating God's holy prophets and taking over. Jezebel had her methods of going about this task. When you read her story you will find this to be true, and by the way, you can find her life from beginning to end in 1 Kings 16:30 thru 2 Kings 9:37. As I was saying she was a dangerous woman who was hateful, vile, prideful, seductive, demanding, manipulating, ruthless, confrontational, lying, and highly controlling in her tactics.

A word of warning to the wise, beware of compromise, the devil is willing to offer each and every one of us to a deal. He wants us to agree to some kind of trade-off, an exchange of sorts. We need to remember that we are no match for the devil, if we try and stand against him in our own strength we will surely fall. The Bible says that King Solomon was the wisest man that ever lived, so then you would think that he would be able to match wits with the devil and come out ahead, however, God had warned him earlier in his life and had also appeared to him more than once. His warning was easy to understand and very clear.

1 Kings 11:1-3

King Solomon, loved many foreign women besides Pharaoh's daughter – Moabites, Ammonites, Edomites, Sidonians, and Hittites. They were from nations about which the LORD had told the Israelites, 'You must not intermarry with them, because they will surely turn your hearts after their gods.' Nevertheless, Solomon held fast to them in love. He had seven hundred wives of royal birth and three hundred concubines, and his wives led him astray. As Solomon grew old, his wives turned his heart after other gods, and his heart was not fully devoted to the LORD his God, as the heart of David his father had been. He followed Ashtoreth the goddess of the Sidonians, and Molek the detestable god of the Ammonites. So Solomon did evil in the eyes of the LORD; he did not follow the LORD completely, as David his father had done.

Wow! can you see the connections? Out of all the other so-called gods I underscored a certain false deity of the Sidonians just to point out that this was the one and the same false deity that Jezebel had worshiped and served during her time. I think we can all learn from these stories because we can see how things worked out for them from beginning to end, let's not make the same mistakes that these people made, for they will cost us dearly if we choose to give ourselves over to the devil the same way they did.

Jesus said something very interesting along this point. You will find it in the gospel of Matthew.

Matthew 8:36-37

For what will it profit a man if he gains the whole world, and loses his own soul? Or what will a man give in exchange for his soul?

Even though Jezebel was a wicked person we need to come to grips with the fact that God loved her. Sometimes I meet people that seem to be so far gone and lost in all types of sins that it seems like there is absolutely no hope for them at all, it would be wise for us to realize that no matter how far or how deep a person may go into sin God's love and great power is more than able to reach them and set them free. This is of great encouragement to me personally because I have been tempted at times to think that there is absolutely no hope for them at all.

The Bible makes this very clear. I like the way the Amplified Bible says it.

Romans 5:20

But where sin increased and abounded, grace (God's unmerited favor) has surpassed it and increased the more and superabounded.

Let's go back to King Solomon, the bible says that Solomons' heart was turned away from the Lord to serve other gods. How could this possibly happen? Really it's very simple. God requires that we give him first place in our lives and he will never settle for second place. When we choose to please others rather than pleasing God, we make a serious mistake. When we bow our wills and our knees to anything else other than God we are taken over by the evil that lies within whatever we submit to. When we disobey a God who is all knowing and all powerful to capitulate or surrender to a lesser and pathetic false god we become their slaves, we then set our lives on a course where we will begin reaping the pains, sufferings, and agonies of our choices.

King Solomon did exactly this. He disobeyed God's commands and took for himself as many wives as he desired. In the process of time he ended up honoring his wives above his Lord and they turned his heart away from God.

As an old man we see a different man altogether,this once wise and powerful king who loved God with all of his heart who in the beginning had offered God a thousand burnt offerings of his love and devotion that pleased God so much that he appeared to Solomon and said to him ***"Ask for whatever me for whatever you want and I will give it to you." 2 Chronicles 1:6-7***

As I was saying we see an entirely different man altogether. In Solomons old age is the portrait of emptiness, disillusionment, and disappointment who then records what is happening in his heart as he put his pen to write the book we know as **Ecclesiastes.**

This book actually means (The Preacher). Solomon at this point in his life has many proclamations that are very depressing, to say the least. His expressions are framed by words like "vain", "futile", "empty", "meaningless", "temporary", "fleeting", or even a "mere breath", his view at this point is depressing and sad as he says that both wise and foolish people end in death.

A life is a terrible thing to waste and I am sad to say that King Solomon found himself at that place in his life. All because he allowed himself to be deceived. It is so important to guard our hearts against anything that would lead us astray.

I promised you a look at another woman who had a creepy and I must say strange coincidence with Jezebel. You will find her in the New Testament with another prophet that resembles The prophet Elijah quite remarkably.

Luke 3:19-20

But when John rebuked Herod the tetrarch because of his marriage to Herodias, his brother's wife, and all the other evil things he had done, Herod added this horrible deed to them all: He locked John up in prison.

Now here is another woman who was as ruthless as Jezebel herself. He name was Herodias. She was the granddaughter of Herod the Great. She was first married to Herod Philip, son of Herod the Great. To make a long story short, she leaves her husband to marry up with Herod Antipas which by the way John the Baptist saw this as an unlawful union. John told him very bluntly ***"It is not lawful for you to have your brother Philip's wife".***

This made Herodias very angry and she behaved as that wicked woman Jezebel did in the courts of King Ahab. Zondervan wrote an article on this dangerous woman. The title of this amazing story is "The Woman Responsible for the Murder of a Preacher" This is an excerpt from it.

Herodias' Old Testament counterpart was Jezebel. What Herodias was to Herod, Jezebel was to Ahab. Both Ahab and Herod were wicked, and in both cases, the woman was more wicked. Both Jezebel and Herodias fostered hate that became deadly against a prophet of God. Jezebel hated Elijah and sought to kill him—Herodias hated John the Baptist, the New Testament Elijah, and succeeded in his murder. What was the end of Herodias? Since she was the source of Herod's sin, Herodias also became the source of his shame. According to Josephus, Herodias' ambition was the ruin of Herod. Jealous of the power of Agrippa her brother, she prodded Herod to demand of Caligula, the emperor, the title of king. Agrippa saw to it that this demand was refused, and Herod was banished and ended his days in shame and exile. The pride of Herodias forced her to be faithful to her husband in the disgrace and misfortune she herself had caused.

Need I say more on this matter? *I don't really think I do, I believe you can see the resemblance in the hearts of these two diabolical women. One final note and warning concerning our own hearts would be that we really need to guard our hearts. No one else is going to guard your heart, the responsibility is yours and yours alone. Proverbs 4:23 says*
"Above everything else guard your heart,
because from it flow the springs of life".

*You see Jesus said "**For out of the heart come evil thoughts—murder, adultery, sexual immorality, theft, false testimony, slander. These are what defile a person**". Matthew 15:19-20*

Your heart is a precious thing and a terrible thing to waste, so make every effort to keep it safe from every kind of evil.

A Man Who Had A Heart Transplant

What does it mean to have a good heart or even better what does it mean to have a healthy heart? The reason I ask this is because we live in a day and age where a good heart seems to be lacking in so many folks. I believe however that there is a remnant of people that may have such a thing as a good heart. I do not consider myself to be a pessimist but I believe the bible is clear on this matter, did you know that there will be many more people that will go into eternity without God than those who will go to heaven with God. As hard as this may sound to all of us this is what Jesus was saying when he said, ***"For wide is the gate and broad is the road that leads to destruction, and many enter through it".But the gateway to life is very narrow and the road is difficult, and only a few ever find it.***

Going back to having a good heart. I'm not sure you are aware of this but in order to have a good heart, you are going to need to receive this kind of heart from God himself. No one is born with a "good heart, we may wish were, but the truth is, we are not. In fact, the bible says,

> ***"The heart is deceitful above all things,***
> ***And desperately wicked;***
> ***Who can know it?***
> ***Jeremiah 17:9***

The Amplified Bible says it this way.

The heart is deceitful above all things, and it is exceedingly perverse and corrupt and severely, mortally sick! Who can know it [perceive, understand, be acquainted with his own heart and mind]?

The story I am about to tell you is going to shock you on many levels because of the content of this one man's life, so let's begin. Once upon a time there lived a good King who loved and honored God, In fact, he was one of the most spiritual kings that the ancient Israelites ever had, his name was Hezekiah. His name means ***"Strengthened by God"***. *Hezekiah purified and repaired the Temple, cleared out all its idols, and reformed the priesthood.In an effort to do away with what he considered idolatry from his kingdom. King Hezekiah also destroyed all the high places.*

Hezekiah had a son by the name of ***Manasseh.*** This interesting person was everything his father was not. He was all for pagan worship and his father king Hezekiah detested any that had to do with pagan worship. He re-instituted pagan worship and reversed the religious reforms made by his father Hezekiah. Manasseh had an evil heart that caused him to turn away from God. This prince had every opportunity and every advantage to be an even better king than his father but he made the choice to take the lowest road possible in his life of rebellion. He was even known to sacrifice his own little children to the devil and the way that the did this despicable act was even more atrocious and barbaric.

2 Chronicles 33:6 ISV

He burned his sons as an offering in the Ben-Hinnom Valley, practiced fortune-telling, witchcraft, sorcery, and communicated with mediums and spiritists. He did a lot of things that the LORD considered to be evil, thus provoking him.

Manasseh was determined to go down in flames by giving himself to every evil practice imaginable and if this was not bad enough he took it upon himself to lead the whole nation into these same evils. An evil heart will take you to the lowest of lows, in Manasseh's case the bible says that he even made Judah and the inhabitants of Jerusalem go astray *and* to do worse than the heathen, whom the LORD had destroyed before the children of Israel.

But Manasseh's kingdom was overthrown by another nation, he was captured and put in prison. And while he was there, Manasseh did something no one could ever have expected: he turned to God. The Bible says, "In his distress, he sought the favor of the Lord his God and humbled himself greatly" (2 Chronicles 33:12). As a result, God forgave him, and also gave him a second chance by restoring him to his throne. Afterward,

Manasseh demonstrated his change of heart by reversing his evil policies.

What is the point? Simply this: God can forgive and change even the most evil person. Pray for your cousin, that God will break through the hardness of his heart and show him his need of Christ. And pray too that you may be an example to him of Christ's love and mercy.

(Send your queries to "My Answer," c/o Billy Graham, Billy Graham Evangelistic Association, 1 Billy Graham Parkway, Charlotte, N.C., 28201; call 1-(877) 2-GRAHAM, or visit the Web site for the Billy Graham Evangelistic Association: http://www.billygraham

New Living Translation

Luke 8:15King James Version (KJV)

15 But that on the good ground are they, which in an honest and good heart, having heard the word, keep it, and bring forth fruit with patience.

Matthew 12:35King James Version (KJV)

35 A good man out of the good treasure of the heart bringeth forth good things: and an evil man out of the evil treasure bringeth forth evil things.

King James Version (KJV)

A Story About A Man With An Empty Heart

Balaam was a man that found himself caught between a rock and a hard place. What I mean is that he found himself caught between God and a very persistent KIng. Some say Balaam was a prophet of God and others consider him nothing more than just a prophet for hire.

Whatever he was we know that he must have had some reputation among the people of his day. You can find his story in the book of Numbers chapters 22-24. There was a king of the area of Moab by the name of Balak who was terrified over the fact that the Israelites who were being led by Moses had come into his land to possibly take over and settle in, at least that is what he may have thought.

King Balak sent a delegation to Balaam saying something very interesting. Numbers 22:6 "So <u>come right now</u> and curse this person for me because there are too many of them for me to handle. Perhaps

I will be able to strike them down and drive them out of the land since I know that whoever you bless is blessed and whomever you curse is cursed"

Apparently, It seems that Balaam had himself a reputation of some sort, perhaps he was summoned from time to time by the people in his area to either call a blessing or some kind of curse on someone or maybe some group of people. We have to ask ourselves, who was this so-called prophet anyway? Was he really even a prophet at all.

Well, there is one thing for sure, Balaam was not an Israelite. Here is an interesting thing to consider, Balaams name actually means "***not of the people***".

The bible says that Balaam practiced divination, which by the way was prohibited by God. ***Deuteronomy 18:10 "There shall not be found among you anyone that uses divination or an observer of times or an enchanter."*** Divination is nothing more than a person who practices the occult.

From ancient times, people have used divination to gain knowledge of the future and many times as a way to make money, especially during the time of Balaam. Pagan practices such as divination were very common. Balaam came highly recommended it seems, at least Balak the king of Moab thought so.

The Israelites seemed to be a great threat to this king from the day he encountered this great multitude. Fear struck his heart and the hearts of his people because they had heard the news about these peculiar people who were on their way somewhere devouring kings and taking over their lands along the way. In reality however the Israelites were really no threat at all to this king in particular, in fact, God himself had told the Israelites not to do any harm to these people of Moab because they were the Israelites relatives thru their descendant Lot who happened to be the nephew of Abraham.

Deuteronomy 2:9

"Then the Lord said to me, "Do not harass the Moabites or provoke them to war, for I will not give you any part of their land. I have given Ar to the descendants of Lot as a possession."

So you see Balak really didn't have anything to worry about. It's never a good idea to jump to conclusions, we can get into a lot of trouble just like Balak was getting himself into. I don't believe Balak knew anything about what God had said to Moses but I am sure of one thing when you get hasty you can make some big mistakes.

Numbers 22:2-4

"Now Balak son of Zippor saw all that Israel had done to the Amorites, and Moab was terrified because there were so many people. Indeed Moab was filled with dread because of the Israelite's" The Moabite's said to the elders of Midian, "This hoard is going to lick up the everything around us, as an ox licks up the grass of the field."

What would it look like to you if you looked down on a vast amount of people that numbered over two million if you can see such a crowd that would fill a quadrangle twelve miles by twelve miles square? This is mind-boggling, to say the least. King Balak was a man driven by fear and that is why he was willing to seek out what he thought was the best solution for overcoming this seemingly large so-called threat to his kingdom. Balaam was offered a large amount of money to curse the Israelites. Here we have a devilish duo. A king driven by fear and desperation and also a false prophet driven by the love of money and unjust gain. 2 Peter 2:14-15 says, "They have their heart's expertly trained in greed, They are doomed to a curse.

They have forsaken the right way and are gone astray following the way of Balaam the son of Bosor who loved the wages of unrighteousness". Together these two will anger God Almighty and bring heaven to earth as God steps in and brings only blessings on this whole debacle. You see when it comes to God's blessing a person or a people, there is no devil in hell that can successfully bring a curse that will conquer or overcome in any way. As you read this incredible story in the bible you will soon see that God himself will have the last word. The apostle Peter speaks to us about a way that we must all avoid. He refers to it as the way of Balaam. What is it the way of Balaam anyway?

Well to answer that we would need to look deep into Balaam's heart and soul. You see when the first messengers came to his home with the request of king Balak to place a curse on God's people, God comes on the scene by asking Balaam, "Who are these men?". After Balaam explains, God explicitly tells him not to go with them. This amazing moment of having almighty

God actually speak to him should have placed a great fear and reverence in Balaam's heart.

If we look closely we can see that Balaam was not willing to take no for an answer. He told the messengers he was not able to go with them but in Balaam's heart, he still desired to go. He was set in his heart to go with them and God could see that. His way was not in line with God's. We must always remember that God looks on our hearts, he knows us inside and out. If we are set in our own ways with no interest in changing whatsoever, if our hearts are determined and have our minds bent on doing what is wrong we will absolutely not come out ahead in our lives.

God's word is very clear and really not difficult at all to understand. ***Isaiah 55:8. "For my thoughts are not your thoughts, neither are your ways my ways says the Lord".*** If we are wise we will make his thoughts our thoughts and make his ways our own. Balaam was trying to find a way to change God's mind instead of changing his own and it made the Lord very angry the bible says.

It's very interesting that when the second group of messengers came seeking Balaam, God allows him to go with them. Believe it or not, God will allow us to have our own way at times, this happens many times to our own hurt but he does this only when we are stubborn, defiant and headstrong. An unwillingness to bend to God's will and purposes will get us nowhere with the Lord? There is a story in the book of Genesis about a man by the name of Jacob. You can find it in ***Genesis 32:24-31***

This man just had to have his own way in his life, in fact, his name actually means "deceiver," Jacob was a very determined person and at times could be a ruthless man and a manipulator. Nevertheless, this particular person had a heart for God so I believe God was willing to work with him. Jacob was brought to a difficult place in his life where God shows up and Jacob finds himself in a wrestling match with the Almighty himself. You may find this hard to believe but Jacob was actually winning.

Up to that time, Jacob lived his life according to his own ways and because of that, he was going to find himself getting into all kinds of trouble. At this time in his life, he was hard pressed between two people in his life, one was his father-in-law Laban and his very angry brother Esau who he had deceived years earlier and had vowed to kill him. Laban was also very angry and had just caught up with Jacob and his fleeing family. If God wouldn't have intervened he may have killed Jacob. Jacob was stressed out, to say the least only to receive news that Esau his brother was on his way to meet him from another direction bringing four hundred armed men with him.

That night Jacob was out of answers, his ways had caught up with him and the bible says that Jacob was greatly distressed. We need to realize that without God we are left to our own resources, it really is a travesty when we are left to our own resources. Our resources are a poor substitute for living a successful life. Jacob was about to finally cave in, his life's circumstances had finally reduced him to utter helplessness.

Jacob needed God as he had never needed him before. Life is funny like that, and if you are honest you will have to admit that there are times when we are in need of something, let's say for instance it is something financial. So then we pray, however way at the back of our minds we already have some things kind of figured out. We reason in our minds that if for some unseen reason God doesn't come through for us we can always use one of our credit cards or something else. Self-sufficiency is the default setting of every human being on the face of the planet.

To be self sufficient sounds like a noble and honorable thing but we need to always remember that God desires for us to only find our sufficiency in him. ***2 Corinthians 3:5 "Not that we are sufficient of ourselves to think anything as of ourselves, but our sufficiency is of God"*** Anytime we start thinking that we really don't need God and we can handle things ourselves we are setting ourselves up for some real eye-opening experiences. Jacob was at one of those places in his life.

In his desperation and hopelessness Jacob cried out to the Lord for help but this time he was coming to God wide-eyed probably feeling lost and hopeless at this point, but being the person we know as Jacob the "Manipulator" to be, he is by this time beginning to feel that his circumstances have gotten out of his control and he is still trying to maneuver his way out of this whole thing. Left all alone as he sent everyone else before him he has a unique encounter with God. The bible says he was met by a man that confronted him. Jacob comes face to face with God. I believe with all my heart that God was challenging Jacob to change his way of doing things in his life. I believe that God was no longer willing to stand on the sidelines and allow Jacob to run his own life according to his own craftiness. The bible says that they wrestled all night long until the breaking of day.

When the Lord saw that he was not prevailing against Jacob he touched the hollow of his thigh and put it out of joint. God then said "Let me go" and Jacob said to the Lord," I will not let you go unless you bless me". Here is where it gets good, the Lord asks Jacob for his name. You know as well as I do that the Lord already knew what Jacob's name was, however, the Lord was bringing Jacob to a place where he needed to admit what kind of person he had become, so Jacob said, "My name is Jacob, which actually meant deceiver, manipulator, supplanter or you could say, claim jumper, someone who is right at your heels so as to take advantage of you. In other words, Jacob had to admit what type of person he was and I'm sure it wasn't easy, just like it's not easy for us at times when we have to admit something about ourselves that isn't pretty. There are areas in the bible where we are told that we need to Judge ourselves or humble ourselves. No One is able to do this for us, we need to do these things ourselves. Taking responsibility is difficult at times, but if we are ever going to grow or change for the better we will have to do this. Once Jacob admitted to God what kind of man he was, God was able to bless him. The blessing changed his identity, he was given a new name, God said to him " You shall no longer be called Jacob but instead you shall be called Israel, which meant, (God Prevails). When we allow God to rule in our lives we actually benefit from his leadership. It is to our advantage that we allow God to have first place in our lives. Listen to what Jesus said, Matthew 16:25 "Whoever wants to save his life will lose it, but whoever loses his life for my sake shall save it".

It's really amazing how we can mess things up when we are in control, and even when we really think that we are in total control of our lives we are really just fooling ourselves. There is a devil out there bent on destroying our lives. His sole purpose is to steal, kill and destroy, so of course, he is going to allow a person to think that they themselves are in total control of their destiny. So then, if God himself is not given the opportunity to rule in our lives we are going to be led astray to follow this world system and what it stands for. If we would just open our eyes we would be able to see that this world and all that is happening in it is just simply out of control. Almost everything in our society is all out of sync with how God has designed it. God says to us, get married, no we say, we'll just live together, God says homosexuality is unacceptable so we as a society say, we will just accept it as an alternative lifestyle, and if you want to get married, you just go right ahead and by the way, may I just say that even though homosexual marriages are being performed and marriage licenses are being handed out, they are null and void in the eyes of God. A true marriage between a man and a woman is actually performed by God himself. Jesus said," **A man will leave his father and mother and be united with his wife, and the two will become one flesh. So they are no longer two, but one flesh. Therefore, what God has joined together, man must never separate." Matthew 19:5-6**

So then, if God has not joined two people together in marriage they are not truly married. I could go on and on but I think you get the point. The Bible calls the devil the ruler of the darkness of this world, or you could say this world system.

Jacob was a self-willed person until God changed the direction of his life. Well, let's get back to this man Balaam. Balaam wasn't willing to bend, he had set himself on a road of destruction and greed was his guide, greed was his escort and greed was his way of blessing himself or you could say, helping himself. On his way, he ran into some problems with his transportation. Balaam had a donkey that had been a faithful companion to his master, at least that's what the donkey said.

Numbers 22:22-34

"But God was angry because he was going, and the angel of the LORD took his stand in the way as an adversary against him. Now he was riding on his donkey and his two servants were with him. When the donkey saw the angel of the LORD standing in the way with his drawn sword in his hand, the donkey turned off from the way and went into the field; but Balaam struck the donkey to turn her back into the way. Then the angel of the LORD stood in a narrow path of the vineyards, with a wall on this side and a wall on that side. When the donkey saw the angel of the LORD, she pressed herself to the wall and pressed Balaam's foot against the wall, so he struck her again. The angel of the LORD went further and stood in a narrow place where there was no way to turn to the right hand or the left. When the donkey saw the angel of the LORD, she lay down under Balaam; so Balaam was angry and struck the donkey with his stick. And the LORD opened the mouth of the donkey, and she said to Balaam, "What have I done to you, that you have struck me these three times?" Then Balaam said to the donkey, "Because you have made a mockery of me! If there had been a sword in my hand, I would have killed you by

now." The donkey said to Balaam, "Am I not your donkey on which you have ridden all your life to this day? Have I ever been accustomed to do so to you?" And he said, "No."

Then the LORD opened the eyes of Balaam, and he saw the angel of the LORD standing in the way with his drawn sword in his hand, and he bowed all the way to the ground. The angel of the LORD said to him, "Why have you struck your donkey these three times? Behold, I have come out as an adversary because your way was contrary to me. "But the donkey saw me and turned aside from me these three times. If she had not turned aside from me, I would surely have killed you just now, and let her live." Balaam said to the angel of the LORD, "I have sinned, for I did not know that you were standing in the way against me".

God was going to use Balaam to pronounce some very interesting blessings on his people, in fact, one of those blessings is what I believe the Magi or you could call them, (The wise men of the Christmas story). These interesting men used what came out as a blessing as a reference to seeking Jesus in Bethlehem.

Numbers 24:17

"I see Him, but not now; I behold Him, but not near; A Star shall come out of Jacob; A Scepter shall rise out of Israel".

You will have to read the complete story yourself, but in a nutshell, every time Balaam stands up to pronounce a curse on Gods people in accordance with Balaks wishes, only blessing and good proceed forth from his lips. This whole scene just frustrates king Balak to no end. From every direction possible from one mountain top to the next, king Balak and this so-called prophet position themselves to pronounce some kind of curse on Israel. But God turns it into a blessing. Just remember this, If you belong to God, no matter what the devil may intend for evil, God is able to work it out for good, with God on your side you just cannot fail. Well, when it was all said and done king Balak went his way and Balaam went another, however, there is an interesting turn of events when Balaam gets an evil idea that is recorded not too long afterward in the bible. Jesus gives us some insight in the book of Revelations as to what Balaam did to bring a curse upon the Israelites, actually, the Israelites ended up cursing themselves but it was Balaams doing that had everything to do with it. Balaam counseled king Balak to present the Israelite men with the opportunity to commit fornication with women from Moab and get involved with idol worship. His counsel was his way of receiving king Balak's reward. I would encourage you to read these scriptures in the bible that will give you a better understanding of Balaams wickedness. This scripture speaks about something called the doctrine of Balaam.

Revelation 2:14

"But I have a few things against thee because thou hast there them that hold the doctrine of Balaam, who taught Balak to cast a stumbling block before the children of Israel, to eat things sacrificed unto idols, and to commit fornication".

Balaam just had to have his way. Here we have a man that has had incredible encounters with God but yet he seems untouched. How has God moved in your life? Have you allowed his touch on your life to change you and transform you?

Bible stories like these can have a life-changing effect on your life because they are filled with tremendous examples of how to live and how not to live. No person sets out to ruin their lives, but yet this is exactly what happens to many people, they just simply refuse to surrender their lives to God. The wisest thing that we can do is yield to God, otherwise, we become a candidate for a life of much sorrow and pain.

Well, Balaam ends up never being able to enjoy his Ill-gotten gain, the Bible called it "wages of unrighteousness".

2 Peter 2:15

"They have forsaken the right way and gone astray, following the way of Balaam the son of Beor, who loved the wages of unrighteousness"; not to long afterward Balaam was killed along with the enemies of Gods people.

His epitaph is written in three places in the new testament. The apostle Peter speaks about people who are following in the steps of Balaam.

2 Peter 2:15

"They have forsaken the right way and gone astray, following the way of Balaam the son of Beor, who loved the wages of unrighteousness";

Jude 1:11

"Woe to them! For they have gone in the way of Cain, have run greedily in the error of Balaam for profit, and perished in the rebellion of Korah".

Revelation 2:14

"But I have a few things against you because you have there those who hold the doctrine of Balaam, who taught Balak to put a stumbling block before the children of Israel, to eat things sacrificed to idols, and to commit sexual immorality".

This is a sad ending, to say the least, Balaam a man with an empty heart perishes with his money. Its recorded in the book of Joshua

Joshua 13:22

"The children of Israel also killed with the sword Balaam the son of Beor, the soothsayer, among those who were killed by them".

A True Story About A Man That Opened His Heart to The Evil One

Now here is an incredible story about a man by the name of Judas, I'm sure that by now you may recognize this well-known name that I am referring to. This man is none other than ***Judas Iscariot*** himself, the man who betrayed Jesus Christ the Son of God. I don't know how much you know about this man, but I can tell you this one thing for sure, this must be one of the most tragic stories in the bible.

The history of Judas short life portrays a dismal ending of a human life that might have otherwise been honored by God since he was a chosen disciple of Jesus himself. The hatred and repugnance which followed him through the many centuries since that time unto this very day should serve as a lesson and a warning to all who like Judas himself would betray and treat with contempt such a sacred and holy trust.

We can learn some things about this man's life that may be very helpful in our own personal lives. Judas made some extremely bad decisions and some very terrible miscalculations in his life that were going to cost him dearly in the days to come.

The book of Proverbs speaks to us in various ways and one of the things we can learn from it is the fact that a wise person makes it a point to learn from other people's mistakes. What can we learn from this man's life? As we consider the life that Judas chose to live we can see that God was already at work to set this man on the right track, just by simply looking at his very name which by the way meant "He (God) shall be praised". His very name was already pointing him in the right direction so that he could bring God praise, glory and honor.

Another thing we can be sure of is that Judas certainly never lived up to his name, for we know that he went down in history as the man who betrayed Jesus Christ. He is the man that Jesus spoke of when he said "**Woe unto that man by whom the Son of man is betrayed, it would have been better that this man would have never been born**" ***Matthew 26:24***

Jesus knew what lay ahead for Judas, Jesus knew all along what was in the heart of Judas just like he knows what is in our hearts and in our minds. Nevertheless, Jesus chose Judas to be one of his disciples, one of his very own. I think that it is important to understand something before we go on and that is this, Jesus loved Judas just as much as he did any of the other of his disciples and just knowing the character of Jesus I'm sure that he gave Judas every opportunity to make the right choices he needed to make in his life.

God treats each one of us the same way. We all have God-given opportunities to make good decisions and the right choices for our lives. Even though it was prophesied in scripture that Judas would commit this unspeakable and heinous crime of betraying God's only Son. God gave Judas a front row seat in the ministry of Jesus and because of that Judas was privileged to experience the wonders of a loving and kind-hearted God. He saw the dead raised back to life, along with the sick, the lame and the blind. Judas probably saw just about every sick and horribly diseased person you could ever imagine come running, hobbling and many times even being carried by their loved ones from every town around with the hopes of seeing Jesus. He saw time and time again the dying and even the dead laid before the feet of Jesus. Without a doubt, I am sure he had so many eye-widening experiences. Judas was able to see the power of God first hand and up close. This man experienced miracle after miracle of how people's lives can be changed by a loving and merciful God and we cannot forget the time that Jesus sent out his disciples two by two (Judas included) after giving them the power to heal every manner of disease and cast out demons.

Yet for some reason, he chose to go his own way and turn against Jesus. Listen to this, amazing passage of scripture that spoke of Judas Iscariot many years before it took place, ***"He who eats bread with me has lifted up his heel against me" John 13:18***

It is very interesting to see that the scripture or bible prophecy that Jesus used was from the book of **Psalms 41:9 "Yes mine own familiar friend in whom I trusted, which did eat my bread has lifted up his heel against me".** Jesus only quoted the second half of that specific scripture. He left out "***my own familiar friend"***. Judas did eat from the same bread and food that

Jesus also ate from, I believe close fellowship is inferred here however I believe that Judas never really got close enough to Jesus to become a good friend in his own heart. How sad is that? Jesus said, ***"he who eats bread with me has lifted his heel against me".***

Now, why would Judas do such a thing? Why would Judas turn on his heel and just decide to leave Jesus behind? It's very interesting this phrase, **(Lifted up his heel against me)**. It is used as an illustration of someone who rapidly leaves someone or something behind because of something they are deeply disapproving of. Jesus called Judas by name to walk with him and be one of his own close followers. He taught him about the kingdom of God and gave him a specific task in his ministry. I can't find another disciple in the group that was blessed with a distinct position as Judas was, for you see Jesus made Judas the treasurer! This truly is a big deal because Jesus knew what was in Judas heart and despite that he still gave him this great and awesome responsibility. I have always said, in my opinion of course, that God is a God who believes in people. He believes the best about us, even with all our failures and quirks, even when we let him down at times. God entrusts each one of us with such priceless opportunities, that if we choose to take advantage of them could change our lives for the better. Jesus Christ placed his trust in this man Judas when he gave him the responsibility of the finances of his ministry. Remember the prophecy "My **own familiar friend in whom I *trusted"***

You probably remember this story, it's found in John 12:3-6 A woman by the name of Mary took a pound of very expensive perfume and anointed the feet of Jesus while wiping his feet with her hair. Judas Iscariot, one of his disciples spoke up immediately and said, "why wasn't this perfume not sold for 300 denarii (about a year's wages) and the money given to the poor? Judas said this not because he cared for the poor but because he was a thief. He was in charge of the moneybag and would steal what was put into it."

Even though I believe, Jesus knew Judas had a serious character flaw in this area, he still entrusted him with this part of his ministry. Judas, however, betrayed that trust, which by the way would eventually end up paving a road in his life that would lead him in a direction that would have more serious and dangerous consequences in the not so distant future. Judas was a thief the bible says; did he not stop to think that Jesus might know this little secret of his? Is it possible that Judas thought that maybe he was getting away with it? On the other hand, could it even be possible that Judas may have really never believed deep in his heart that Jesus was God, the Messiah himself? Whatever the reason may have been, Judas had some internal struggles that he was going to need to deal with.

We all have similar struggles from time to time in hearts and in our minds. We also need to deal with whatever weaknesses we may have because if we do not take steps to overcome those weaknesses those same weaknesses will overcome us.

Judas did a great evil against the Lord Jesus Christ. I'm not talking about just the fact that he was taking what did not belong to him from time to time. I am talking about something much more serious, like selling Jesus out. This part of the story concerning this man Judas Iscariot that you are about to hear has been told and retold for over two thousand years causing people from all walks of life to wonder on how this dastardly and despicable deed could actually be committed by one of his very own disciples.

Judas, the bible says, sold Jesus to the evil religious leaders of his day. Listen to what Judas said to them,* "and he said to them, what will you give me if I will deliver him unto you? and they made a deal with him for thirty pieces of silver".*Matthew 26:15

Judas, I believe is what many would call an opportunist, the bible says this in a very clear term. The following verses of this same passage of scripture say that Judas after he had made this under the table deal with the religious leaders, looked for an opportunity from that time on so that he could deliver Jesus unto them. The definition of an opportunist is a person who exploits circumstances to gain the advantage of anyone or anything. In other words, this person will do anything for selfish gain.

Thirty pieces of silver, as the bible puts it, was probably the lowest price that a person could be sold for in those days as a slave. Make it a point to never forget what I am about to tell you right now, the bible is very clear on this. The word of God says, "**The love of money is the root of all evil**". **1 Timothy 6:10** You could say it this way, the love of money is the root of all kinds of evil.

I know that you have probably heard this before, but many times this verse of scripture is sadly misquoted. You see it doesn't say that money is the root of all evil, it says, "**The love of money is the root of all evil**".

The Tale of Two Masters

Jesus said, "**Be careful you cannot serve two masters, for you will either hate the one and love the other. Or you will hold true to one and despise the other, you cannot serve God and money**". ***Matthew 6:24***

Money in itself is not good or evil, it really depends very much on the person using it. If a good person uses money they will use it for good purposes, but if an evil person uses money they will use it for evil purposes.

A person begins to run into problems when they start to develop some level of devotion towards lt before they know it they find themselves developing a love for it. You see when a person begins to make money the most important thing in their lives they will pursue it at any cost and eventually they will begin serving money itself. Money then becomes their master and the truth of the matters is that they will soon find themselves doing anything for this newly found master (Money). Judas is proof of this, it wasn't long before he found himself saying to those who hated Jesus "What ***will you give me if I deliver him unto you?"***

The apostle Paul said something very interesting in Colossians 3:5 "Covetousness **is idolatry".** To covet something as the apostle Paul describes here means that you desire something else other than God. God is the one who should always and always come first in our lives, but when we begin to love and seek, or you could say desire things to the degree that they begin to take preeminence in our hearts and lives we have stepped into something called idolatry.

Idolatry is worshiping something above or instead of God himself. People from every walk of life struggle at times with this sin called covetousness. In Exodus 20:17, which by the way is the last on the list we call the Ten Commandments, God commands us not covet. **"You shall not covet your neighbor's house, you shall not covet your neighbor's wife nor his manservant, nor his maidservant, nor his donkey, nor his ox, nor anything that belongs to your neighbor"** It's interesting on how many of the ten commandments deal with outward expressions of sin towards God or our neighbor, but covetousness deals with what we as human beings experience in our thoughts and our hearts.

For example, one of the commandments deals with the outward sin of adultery, this commandment called covet deals with the strong desire for adultery. Another commandment deals with the outward expression of stealing or thievery. This commandment God calls coveting deals with the strong desire to have what does not belong to you. Judas was going to have to resist this sin of covetousness just the same way we must.

Judas story, as terrible as it is, contains many valuable lessons for each one of us. Here is something else to consider concerning the life of Judas, just because Judas belonged to the group of disciples that followed Jesus everywhere didn't actually make him a disciple at all, at least not in his heart of hearts it didn't. Many people think that just because they go to such and such a church or maybe belong to such and such a group, that this makes them a good person, or maybe a believer, or even a godly person for that matter.

Miscalculations can be very costly in life, I think we can all agree on that. We have all made our share of blunders and errors in our lives because of some miscalculation on our part. Miscalculations and mistakes are born because we have somehow underestimated or overestimated something or someone. Judas, in this case, made a serious error in his life and it ended up costing this poor fellow his soul.

You really need to know this and it would be wise if you would let this go deep within your heart, Jesus knows who truly belongs to him, he can see your heart and he knows who you are truly committed too. ***John 6:70 says "and Jesus answered his disciples and said, have I not chosen you twelve and one of you is a devil"?***

At what we call the last supper Jesus said something that I think shocked all of his disciples. The story goes like this. Jesus took a towel and wrapped it around his waist and began to wash all of his disciple's feet, Peter did not understand at the time what Jesus was doing and declined the offer, however, Jesus assured him that what he was doing he would certainly understand later. Whatever Jesus was doing Peter thought I want it all and he said to Jesus" Don't just wash my feet only but wash my hands and my head as well" then Jesus made this statement", **"Whoever has bathed is entirely clean. He doesn't need to wash himself any further, except for his feet and all you are clean, though not all of you" John 13:10**

I'm sure that Jesus was grieved with the fact that he knew that Judas was going to betray him very soon, in fact, Judas had already committed the devilish act in his heart. All he needed to do was go out and finish his sin and bring it to an end. Jesus as I said, was no doubt filled with much sorrow because of Judas and his choice to come against him. Listen to this, I'm certain it will break your heart as you read it. ***John 13:21 "after saying this Jesus was deeply troubled in spirit and declared solemnly, truly I tell you, one of you will betray me".***

Well, let's go back to where we were earlier. Judas had just left his meeting with his corrupt companions and their evil schemes, on his way to figure out the right time and the right place for this diabolical plans of his. I think you know where this is going. From the time Judas began to take steps in the wrong direction he started to go downhill. Here is an interesting turn of events, after Judas had closed the deal with the religious leaders in betraying Jesus, he did it in a very disturbing manner, he betrayed Jesus with a kiss. The true definition of a kiss is to show love or affection and maybe reverence, however, in this case, it is used as an act of treason to reveal Jesus to the Roman soldiers so that they could arrest him. If you ask me this seems extremely cold-blooded in my estimation, however, if you could see what had happened to Judas just a few hours earlier you would probably understand his situation. **John 13:27 "after Judas had taken the piece of bread from the hand of Jesus, Satan entered him and Jesus told him, do quickly what you are going to do".**

Not too long afterward, Judas began to feel the weight of his decision to betray Jesus. The feelings of guilt and bitter regret began to set in and take hold of his heart, but by that time Satan had a firm grip on his tormented heart. I'm sure there were times that Judas had the power to make good decisions but then there came a time the bible says when Satan entered Judas.

Try as he may he just could not break free. This should be a heads up for all of us. We would be wise to take into consideration what happened to Judas very seriously. If we choose to live our lives closing our eyes to the truth, the day will come when darkness will set in because of our willful blindness. Nobody in their right minds would want to end up like Judas Iscariot. I believe that people have better plans and pursuits for their lives. We need to be wise and be watchful and know that if we give Satan place in any part of our lives he will take advantage of that and begin to develop a **Strong Hold** in that area. In time we will find ourselves in **Bondage** and under his control to him and his evil plans. Jesus is the one who said, ***"He who commits*** *(gives himself over to it)* ***sin is a slave of sin" John 8:34.***

People all over the world are walking in darkness every day. Jesus said that when a person walks in darkness they stumble and fall into all kinds of hardships. In reality, people who walk in darkness end up making all types of costly decisions and if they continue in this kind of living it will cost them everything in the end.

In this story, we see that Judas was beginning to see that he was getting more than he bargained for. Before he realized it, things began to get out of control and there was nothing that he could do about it. Judas went back to the religious leaders and said: ***"I have sinned in that I have betrayed innocent blood, and they said to him, what is that to us, that is your problem, so Judas threw the thirty pieces of silver on the temple floor and went and hung himself". Matthew 27:4***

How tragic is all this? Have you ever heard the expression "too little too late"? This is what happens way too many times in people's lives. They flirt with the devil and play with sin and then they get caught in a trap and a snare that they are helpless to break free from. They try and try but all their efforts as they say, "are too little too late". Without God's intervention, they will suffer the consequences of all their choices.

Always remember that sin will always take you further than you ever intended to go, sin will always cost you more than you ever intended to pay and sin will always keep you longer than you ever wanted to stay. The word of God says that sin will always harden our hearts to what is important and right. In reality, Jesus was the best thing that had ever happened to Judas but he chose to turn his back on him.

Judas goes down in history as the man who turned traitor, he made his choice and he took it to the grave. ***Acts 1:18 "Now this man Judas acquired this field with the reward of his unjust deed,***

(he hung himself) and falling headfirst he burst open in the middle and all of his intestines gushed out".

I ask you, can this story get any more depressing? We all have a choice to make today concerning Jesus, let's not make the wrong one like Judas did. If we choose to reject Jesus as Judas did we will then suffer the consequences, not because God is going to punish us but because we personally have chosen unwisely and foolishly. God has done everything he is going to do so that you can enjoy eternal life. He sent us his son Jesus who took upon himself everyone of our sins and paid for them personally. If a person ends up like this man Judas Iscariot it's not because God didn't try to save us, but it's because we have rejected his goodness and his great kindness, not to mention his great love. The bible says, ***"But God demonstrated his love for us by this fact, while we were yet sinners Jesus Christ died for us" Romans 5:8.*** No One can exchange the truth of God's word for that of a lie and end up coming out ahead in their lives, instead, we find ourselves in all kinds of troubles with no one to blame but ourselves.

Here is one of those truths from God's word. Jesus said in **Mark 8:36-37 "For what will it <u>profit</u> a man if he <u>gains</u> the whole world, and loses his own soul? Or what will a man give in <u>exchange</u> for his soul?**

Milton Keynes UK
Ingram Content Group UK Ltd.
UKHW011124061123
432059UK00001B/77

9 781643 989495